Dive In

Advisory Panel

Cathy Bogusat
Christine Finochio
Mary Francone
Helen Hohmann
Jan McDonald
John McLaughlin
Sharon McPhail
Fiona Morrison
Mary Nall
Lorraine Prokopchuk

Senior Program Consultant

Jennette MacKenzie

Senior Consultants

Sharon Siamon
Frieda Wishinsky

 I(T)P Nelson

an International Thomson Publishing company

Toronto • Albany • Bonn • Boston • Cincinnati • Detroit • London • Madrid • Melbourne
Mexico City • New York • Pacific Grove • Paris • San Francisco • Singapore • Tokyo • Washington

I⟨T⟩P® **International Thomson Publishing**

The ITP logo is a trademark under licence
www.thomson.com

© Copyright ITP®Nelson, 1999

Published by
I⟨T⟩P® Nelson

A division of Thomson Canada Limited
1120 Birchmount Road
Scarborough, Ontario M1K 5G4
www.nelson.com

Printed and bound in Canada
2 3 4 5 6 7 8 9 0/ML/7 6 5 4 3 2 1 0 9 8

Canadian Cataloguing in Publication Data
Main entry under title:
Nelson language arts, [levels A-E]
For use in kindergarten and grade 1.
Contents: Level A. Jump in — Level B. Swing in — Level C. Slide in — Level D. Zoom in — Level·E. Dive in.
ISBN 0-17-618544-5 (level A)   ISBN 0-17-618545-3 (level B)
ISBN 0-17-618546-1 (level C)   ISBN 0-17-618547-X (level D)
ISBN 0-17-618548-8 (level E)

1. Readers (Primary). I. Siamon, Sharon. II. Wishinsky, Frieda

PE1119.N44 1998   428.6   C98-930370-5

Publisher: Mark Cobham
Executive Editor: Susan Green
Production Coordinator: Theresa Thomas
Marketing Manager: Mark Cressman
Art Direction and Design: Sylvia Vander Schee and Peggy Rhodes
Cover Illustration: Amy Wummer

Table of Contents

Across Canada

Yukon

Northwest Territories

Nunavut

British Columbia

Newfoundland

Alberta

Manitoba

Quebec

Ontario

Prince Edward Island

Saskatchewan

Nova Scotia

New Brunswick

Hello. My name is Jessie.
I live in Newfoundland.
Come and visit me.
We'll go fishing in a
Newfoundland fishing boat.

Hello! My name is Denis.
I live in Nova Scotia.
Come and visit me.
I can show you lots of sea birds
that live along the shore.

Hi! My name is Jason.
I live in New Brunswick.
Come and visit me.
We can look for things
along the sea shore.

Hi! My name is Tina.
I live on Prince Edward Island.
Come and visit me.
I'll show you our new bridge.

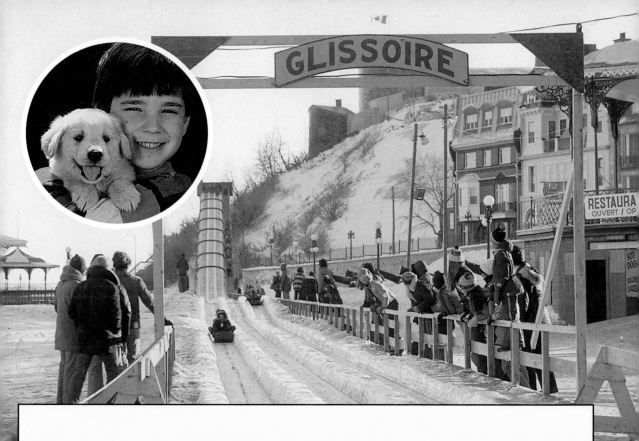

Bonjour! My name is Alain.
I live in Quebec.
Come and visit me in winter.
We can zoom down a snow slide.

Hi! My name is Jenny.
I live in Ontario.
Come and visit me.
We can go to Ottawa and see
the Parliament Buildings.

Hello. My name is Susan.
I live in Manitoba.
Come and visit me.
We can go camping at
Lake Winnipeg.

Hello. My name is David.
Come and visit my big farm
in Saskatchewan.
We can see a lot of sky
from our land.

Hi! My name is Toni.
I live in Alberta.
Come and visit me.
We can go hiking in
the mountains.

Hello. My name is Derek.
I live in British Columbia.
Come and visit me.
We have mountains and islands
and big, big trees!

Hi. My name is Kate.
I live in the Yukon.
Come and visit me.
We have beautiful wildflowers
in the summer.
We can go fishing for Arctic char!

Hello. My name is Mike.
I live in the Northwest Territories.
Come and visit our new
ice rink in Inuvik.
We can play hockey.

Hi. My name is Joanne.
I live in Nunavut.
We are the newest territory in Canada.
I hope you can come and see
how beautiful it is here.

Millie and Patrick

By John McLaughlin

Millie drove a taxi.
Patrick drove a school bus.
Sometimes they passed each other
on the street, and they waved
to each other.

One day, Patrick's school bus broke down.
"Come on, Patrick!" yelled the kids.
"We want to go home!"

"Oh no!" said Patrick.
"I don't know how to fix a bus!"

Then, along came Millie.
"I'm Millie," said Millie.

"I'm Patrick," said Patrick.

"Can I help you?" asked Millie.
"My friends call me *Millie the Fixer*."

"Please do!" said Patrick.
"I don't know how to fix a bus."

Millie looked under the hood.
She fiddled with this and she fiddled with that.
She pulled on this and she pulled on that.
"Let 'er rip, Patrick!" she yelled.

Patrick turned the key and the engine roared.

"Hurray!" yelled the kids.
"We can go home now!"

"Thank you, Millie" said Patrick.
"Maybe some day I will help *you*."

Millie smiled and tooted the horn
as she drove away in her taxi.

One day at the grocery store, Patrick
saw Millie standing all by herself.
"Hello Millie," said Patrick.

"Oh Patrick," said Millie.
"My mother wants an upside down cake
for her birthday. I don't know how to make
an upside down cake!"

Patrick smiled.
"I will help you, Millie," he said.
"My friends call me *Patrick the Baker*."

"Thank you, Patrick!" said Millie.
"You are a good friend."

Cookie Day

by Susan Green

Jon and Kala are making cookies.
Jon's Dad will help. They bring out
all the things they will need and put
them on the kitchen table.

"Read the recipe, Dad," says Jon.

Step 1

Measure flour,
baking soda,
and salt.
Mix them together
in a big bowl.

Jon measures the flour in a cup.
Dad measures the baking soda
and Kala adds salt.
Kala mixes the flour, baking soda,
and salt in a bowl with a big spoon.

Add eggs.
Measure and add
sugar, butter,
and vanilla.

Dad breaks the eggs in another bowl.
Cracking eggs is hard to do. He beats
them and adds them to the sugar, butter,
and vanilla.

Step 3
Beat until smooth.

Then Dad uses the mixer. It goes too fast!

"That isn't part of the recipe," laugh Jon and Kala. "You are a messy baker."

Stir the batter.

Next, they put all the ingredients in the big bowl.

Kala stirs and stirs. Jon stirs too.

Step 5

Add in chocolate chips.

Now it's time for the best part.
Kala adds the chocolate chips.
Jon adds another cup of chocolate chips.
Then he stirs them into the batter.

Step 6
Use a big spoon.
Drop batter on
to baking sheets.

Jon and Kala work together to drop
spoonfuls of batter on to the cookie sheet.
Kala uses a big spoon. Jon holds a little spoon
and scoops out the batter when it sticks.

Dad lets them taste the batter left in the bowl. It tastes good.

"Can we have some more?" asks Jon.

"Wait for the finished cookies," says Dad. "They will taste best."

Step 8

Check to see if cookies are done.

It's hard to wait for the cookies to bake. They smell delicious.

"Can we taste the cookies yet?" asks Kala.

"Soon," says Dad. "Wait just a bit longer."

Step 9
Cool cookies on wire rack.

Finally the cookies are ready.
"You did a good job," says Dad. "The cookies taste great."

"They're crunchy," says Jon.

"The cookies have lots of chocolate chips, too," says Kala. "Now let's share them with our friends."

Cookie Chant

by Sonja Dunn

Cookies on my plate
Cookies on my plate
First there were nine
But now there are eight.
Seven, six, five, four,
Cookies on my plate.

I Fix Phones

by Neita Giles

My name is Neita.
I fix phones.

I drive a truck.
My truck has a ladder on top.
I have tools in my truck.
I use them to fix phones.

I have tools in my belt, too.
I use my tools to put in new phones
and to fix old phones.

Today, I stop my truck outside a house.
I knock on the door.
I show the people my card and tell them,
"I'm here to fix your phone."

Then, I climb the telephone pole.
I wear a hard hat and safety glasses.
I want to see if the phone line is working.

Everything looks fine!
The ground looks far away from up here.

I climb down the pole.
Next, I look at a small box outside the house.
The wires look loose.
I fix the line.

I check the phone again.
I use my special phone.
The line is fixed.
Now the phone works!

The people thank me.
Now the phone is working.
They can call for pizza!

Jack and the Beanstalk

by Sharon Siamon

Jack's mom: Jack, Jack! We have nothing
              to eat.
              We have no money for food.
              You must go and sell the cow.

Jack: I sold the cow, Mom.
I got some magic beans.

Jack's mom: Magic beans! Oh no!
We can't buy food with
magic beans.

(Mom throws beans out the window)

Go to bed now, Jack.

(sound: Cock-a-doodle-doo!)

Jack:	It's morning. I'm so hungry.
Jack's mom:	Look at the beanstalk. It goes right up to the sky!
Jack:	I'm going to climb up and look for food!

Jack's mom:	Be careful! Take this whistle. Blow it if you are in danger.
Jack:	*(Jack blows whistle)*
Jack's mom:	Not now! When you're in danger.
Jack:	Okay, Mom. Here I go.
	(Jack starts to climb)

Jack:	Wow! Look at that big castle! Maybe a giant lives there.
	(sound: Giant's foot steps)
Jack:	Here he comes! I have to run and hide!
	(Jack hides)

Giant:	FEE-FI-FO-FID, I SMELL THE FEET OF A LITTLE KID.
Giant's wife:	There are no kids here. Play with your toy hen. Make it lay a golden egg.
	(sound: Cluck! Cluck! Thump!)
Giant:	Oh boy! Look! Another golden egg!

Giant's wife:	Why don't you take a nap now, dear?
	(sound: Giant snoring)
Jack:	*(Jack comes out)*
	I have to get that hen. Golden eggs will buy a lot of food.
Giant's wife:	The boy needs that hen.

Giant: *(Giant wakes up)*

Hey! You can't take my hen! Bring it back!

Giant's wife: *(Wife opens door for Jack)*

Come here. Quick! Down the beanstalk.

Giant: I've almost got you!

                (Giant and Giant's wife follow)

Giant's wife: Hurry Jack!

Jack: I hope Mom hears the
                whistle.

                (Jack blows whistle)

Jack's mom: Jack is in danger. Where's the axe?

(Mom chops at beanstalk)

Jack: Mom! Wait until I get to the ground!

Jack's mom: Hurry, hurry! The beanstalk is falling!

(Jack, Giant, and Giant's wife fall from beanstalk)

(sound: Crash! Thump!)

Jack's mom: Are you all right, Jack?

Jack: I'm fine. Look what I have.
It's a special hen.
It lays golden eggs.

(sound: Cluck! Cluck! Splat!)

It lays *real* eggs now!

Jack's mom: Real eggs! Now we have food.
Mr. and Mrs. Giant, would
you like to stay for breakfast?

All: FEE-FI-FO-FUM,
PASS THE EGGS, WE'LL ALL HAVE SOME.
FOOD TASTES BEST WHEN SHARED
WITH FRIENDS.
NOW OUR PLAY IS AT AN END.

Make a Rain Jar

What do you need?

- a big jar
- a big tin lid
- a small tin can
- some ice cubes

What do you do?

1. Get an adult to pour hot water in the jar.

2. Put the lid on the jar.

3. Put the tin can on the lid.

4. Fill the can with ice cubes.

What do you see?

The Sea Where I Swim

by Gwen Pascoe

This is the sea where I swim.

This is the sun, shining down,
that warms the sea where I swim.

This is the cloud,
wearing a frown,
that hides the sun,
that warms the sea where I swim.

This is the rain, pattering down,
that falls from the cloud,
that hides the sun,
that warms the sea where I swim.

This is the puddle,
big and round,
that catches the rain,
that falls from the cloud,
that hides the sun,
that warms the sea where I swim.

This is the creek, gurgling down,
that drains the puddle,
that catches the rain,
that falls from the cloud,
that hides the sun,
that warms the sea where I swim.

This is the river, near the town,
that gathers the creek,
that drains the puddle,
that catches the rain, that falls from the cloud,
that hides the sun,
that warms the sea where I swim.

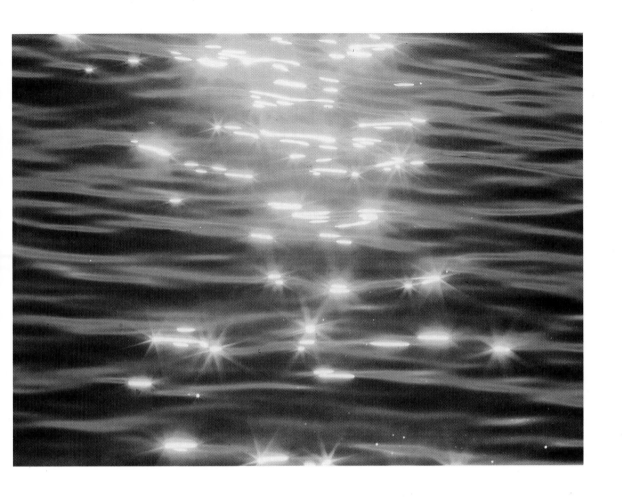

This is the sea,
like a glittering crown,
that meets the river,
that gathers the creek,
that drains the puddle, that catches the rain,
that falls from the cloud,
that hides the sun,
that warms the sea where I swim.

This is the sea where I swim!

Reading

by Marchette Chute

A story is a special thing.
The ones that I have read,
They do not stay inside the book,
They stay inside my head.

Ice Cream

by Marcia Vaughan

Chapter One

It was a hot day at the beach.
Goldsworthy and Mort sat in their chairs
watching the waves roll in.

Goldsworthy sighed, "I would like something
creamy and cold and sweet to eat."

"An ice cream cone is what I'd like.
My favourite flavour is —"

"Wait!" shouted Mort.
He jumped out of his chair.

"Don't tell me. I can guess what your favourite flavour is."

"You can?" asked Goldsworthy.

"Yes," said Mort.

"I am a very good guesser."

Chapter Two

Mort ran across the hot sand to the snack cart. Then he ran back again.

"Here is a chocolate ice cream cone.
Your favourite kind," Mort said proudly.

Goldsworthy did not smile back.
"But Mort," he said, "chocolate is *not*
my favourite flavour."

Mort's whiskers drooped.
"I do not like chocolate
very much myself," he said.

"Don't look so sad," said Goldsworthy. "Chocolate is not my favourite flavour, but I will eat it anyway."

"Do that," grinned Mort, "while I get you a different kind."

"Mort, my favourite kind is —"

Mort put his paws over his ears.
"Don't tell me, Goldsworthy.
I can guess," said Mort.

Chapter Three

Minutes later Mort returned
looking very pleased with himself.

A cone with five scoops of ice cream
wobbled in his fist.

The first scoop was raspberry.
The second scoop was blueberry.
The third scoop was orange swirl.
The fourth scoop was pineapple.
And the fifth scoop was
raisin rocky-road ripple.

"Ho, ho," laughed Mort. "This cone
has to have your favourite flavour."

But Goldsworthy did not laugh.

"No, Mort," he said.
"That cone does *not* have
my favourite flavour on it."

Mort gasped.
"Not one of these is
your favourite flavour?"
Mort asked.

"No," said Goldsworthy.

"Are you sure?" Mort asked.

"*Very* sure," said Goldsworthy.

Mort stared at the ice cream cone.
He watched the ice cream dripping
on to the sand.

"I don't like any of these flavours either,"
he said.

Mort looked like he was
going to cry.

"Don't worry a whisker, Mort,"
said Goldsworthy. "I will eat this
ice cream cone too."

Chapter Four

All afternoon Mort tried to guess
Goldsworthy's favourite flavour
of ice cream.

"Maple nut?"
"Candy corn crunch?"

"Citrus surprise?"
"Bubblegum jumble?

And all afternoon Goldsworthy ate
Mort's mistakes.

The sun was slowly sinking
as Mort bought the last flavour
of ice cream from the snack cart.

Mort was so excited that he did not
watch where he was going.
Thunk!
He tripped on a stick.

Whizz!
Up flew the ice cream.

Plop!
It came down right on top of
an ant hill.

"Jumping jellybeans!" cried Mort. "Goldsworthy's ice cream is covered with hundreds of little black ants."

Chapter Five

Mort felt awful.
He trudged up to Goldsworthy.

He held out the cone with
the bumpy black blobs on it.

"Is this ice cream?" Goldsworthy asked.

Mort nodded.

"Is this plain old everyday
vanilla ice cream?" Goldsworthy asked.

Mort nodded again.

"Is this plain old everyday
vanilla ice cream covered
with hundreds of tiny black ants?"

"Yes," Mort sighed sadly. "It is."

Goldsworthy jumped up and down.
He danced around Mort.
"You are a good guesser, Mort,"
he sang.

"Because my favourite kind of ice cream
is plain old everyday vanilla
covered with ants!"

"Hurray!" cheered Mort.
He pushed the cone into
Goldsworthy's paws.

Suddenly Goldsworthy's face
turned as green as seaweed.
"I am very sorry, Mort,"
said Goldsworthy.

"But my stomach doesn't feel
like any more ice cream today.
You can eat it."

Mort stared at the wiggly black ants.
Mort thought about all the ice cream
that Goldsworthy had eaten for him.

He closed his eyes.
He held his nose.
He popped the ice cream
into his mouth and swallowed it.
Gulp.

"Gosh," said Mort, "that was great.
I think vanilla ice cream
covered with ants is
my favourite flavour, too."
And Mort hurried off
to the snack cart for more.

Acknowledgments

"Across Canada" and "Jack and the Beanstalk" copyright © Sharon Siamon; "Millie and Patrick" copyright © John McLaughlin. "Cookie Day" copyright © Frieda Wishinsky; "Cookie Chant" copyright © Sonja Dunn. "The Sea Where I Swim" text copyright © Gwen Pascoe, 1994. Published by Nelson Australia Pty Ltd in 1994. Reprinted by permission. "Reading" by Marchette Chute from RHYMES ABOUT US, E.P.Dutton, Inc., copyright 1974 by Marchette Chute, reprinted by permission of Mary Chute Smith. "Ice Cream" from GOLDSWORTHY AND MORT—SUMMER FUN. Text copyright © 1990 Marcia Vaughn. Illustrations copyright © 1990 by Linda Hendry.

Illustrations

Kim LaFave, pp.18-25; Per Gurth, pp.26-35; Toni Goffe, p.36; Scott Ritchie, pp.46-57; Sami Suomalainen, p.69; Linda Hendry, pp.70-95.

Photographs

George Hunter/Comstock, pp.5,6,7,16; Bruce Berg/Visuals Unlimited, p.5 (inset); Comstock, pp.6 (inset), 7 (inset), 8 (inset), 9 (inset), 10 (inset), 12 (inset), 14 (inset), 17 (inset), 61, 63; John Sylvester, p.8; J.Jacquemain/Comstock, p.9; Jim Cochrane/The Canadian Tourism Commission, p.10; E.Otto/Comstock, pp.11-12; Marks Product/The Image Bank, p.11 (inset); T.Kitchin/First Light, p.13; Elyse Lewin/The Image Bank, p.13 (inset); K.Nagai/Comstock, p.14; Martin G.Miller/Visuals Unlimited, p.15; McCutcheon/Visuals Unlimited, p.15 (inset); D.Lokey/Comstock, p.16 (inset); William Belsey, p.17; Doug Crawford, pp.37-45; Bob Semple, pp.60, 68; B.Wittman/Comstock, p.62; Tony Freeman/Photo Edit, p.64; H.A.Roberts/E.R.Degginger/Comstock, p.65; Malak/Comstock, p.66; G.Graham/Comstock, p.67.